LOOKING FOR
FLANNEL PAJAMAS

OTHER WORKS BY ADRIENNE RICHARD

FICTION

Pistol (1969)
The Accomplice (1973)
Wings (1974)
Into The Road (1976)

Atlantic Monthly Press – Little, Brown & Company

NON-FICTION

Epilepsy: A New Approach (with neurologist Dr. Joel Reiter)

Prentice Hall Press, 1990.
Paperback edition, Walker and Company, 1995.

POETRY

Originally published in the following journals:

"Waiting" published in the *Connecticut River Review*
by the Connecticut Poetry Society, July/August 2004
"On The Snake River" published in *Fences*
by the Wyoming Poetry Society, 2007.

BIOGRAPHY

Something About The Author, Volume 9, autobiography series,
Joyce Nakamura, Editor.

Published by Gale Research, 1990.

LOOKING FOR FLANNEL PAJAMAS

Selected Poems 1993–2010

For Elena & Scott
Hope you get another laugh
from "Pajamas" p. 102
Merry Christmas 2013
Adrienne Richard
" Pat "

ADRIENNE RICHARD

Inkspiration Media

Looking for Flannel Pajamas: Selected Poems 1993-2010

Published by:
Inkspiration Media
2724 Dorr Avenue, Suite 103
Fairfax, VA 22031
www.InkspirationMedia.com

ISTC: A0320120000B4773
Library or Congress Control Number: 2013904685

Publisher's Cataloging-In-Publication Data
(Prepared by The Donohue Group, Inc.)

Richard, Adrienne.
[Poems. Selections. 2013]
Looking for flannel pajamas : selected poems, 1993-2010 / Adrienne Richard.
p. ; cm.
ISBN-13: 978-1-939319-00-5 (pbk.)
ISBN-10: 1-939319-00-5 (pbk.)
ISBN-13: 978-1-939319-26-5 (hardcover)
ISBN-10: 1-939319-26-9 (hardcover)
1. American poetry. I. Title. II. Title: Poems. Selections. 2013
PS3568.I269 R34 2013
811/.54   2013904685

Book design by Emily Richard Einheit. Text set in Palatino.
Cover design by David Wu, DW Design.
Cover photo of Adrienne Richard on remains of East Beach Road in Westport,
Mass., August 31, 2011, after Tropical Storm Irene swept through area;
AP Photo, The Standard Times of New Bedford by Peter Pereira.
Author photo by Patricia Barry Levy, www.PatriciaBarryLevy.com.
Printed in the United States of America.
Talbots is a registered trademark of the respective owners.

For Jim
1916-1992

CONTENTS

BLUE BONES (1993-1998)

I
In The Press Room । 13

II
Ojai । 15
The Kettle Pond । 16
A Child's History Of Iraq । 17
The Summer House । 18
Liberal, Kansas । 20

III
A Winter Journey । 23
Ear Mountain । 30
Bandelier । 32
Mexico City । 33
Oaxaca । 34
Pulse । 35

IV
Blue Bones । 37
Fly Casting । 38
The Crematory । 39
On The Snake River । 40

ON NECESSITY STREET (1998-2003)

I
On Necessity Street | 45

II
The Ice Forest | 49
From A Winter Night | 50
Spring: New England | 51
Late Spring | 52
The Mailbox | 53
Endangered | 54
In Miniature | 55

III
Walking Sticks | 57
Burying Ground | 58
Battleground | 60
The Buffalo | 61
Two Trees | 62

IV
The Foundryman | 65
For The Love Of Bridges | 66
The Good Times Café | 68
On The Beach | 69
The Blue Crab | 70

RAGS OF TIME (2003-2010)

I
A Book Of Hours ⎮ 75

II
The Abyss ⎮ 79
The Rat Codex A Fragment ⎮ 80
Miriam's Song ⎮ 85
Pilgrims ⎮ 88

III
On My 77th Birthday ⎮ 91
After September 11, 2001 ⎮ 92
September 28, 2001 ⎮ 94
On Turning 80 ⎮ 95
An Octogenarian Considers Forgiveness ⎮ 96
October 31, 2005 ⎮ 97
An Octogenarian Contemplates Being One ⎮ 98
My Eighty-Fifth Waltz ⎮ 99
An Octogenarian Thinks Of Her Future ⎮ 100
An Octogenarian Browses The New Talbots Catalog,
    Looking For Flannel Pajamas ⎮ 102
Heat Wave ⎮ 104

IV
Picasso Eats A Fish ⎮ 107
A Note To William Carlos Williams ⎮ 108
Wordsworth In September ⎮ 109
On A Reading By Adrienne Rich At UMass-Boston ⎮ 110
On Reading Thomas Merton ⎮ 111
For Stanley Kunitz ⎮ 113

About The Poet ⎮ 114

Acknowledgments ⎮ 115

BLUE BONES

1993-1998

I

IN THE PRESS ROOM

My father took me into the ill-lit loft.
Tall, in his dark suit, he introduced me
to the bindery girls sitting at their tables,
swabbing rubber cement on the spines of books,
to the linotypist who set my name backwards
in hot type, to the great presses clanking
in the dim room, to the pressman who stood
beside them as blackened with ink and grease
as the presses themselves, and to the smell –
the smell of printer's ink that pervaded
the loft, a smell so thick and intense that
it entered my nose and my pores and my blood
and my brain, and I knew I wanted to be
where ink met paper for the rest of my life.

II

OJAI

In Ojai, a California valley, at the age of seven
I came upon the landscape of my life
and other deep-dyed instinctual, blood-brain things
that cannot be denied or left behind:

The spreading, black trunked live oaks,
the tan dry grasses, tall when you are seven,
wild oats and anise, the smell of orange groves
everywhere, the ring of pitiless mountains,
the face of Topa Topa rosy at sunset, the sky's turquoise edge.

The white sycamore near the road stretched
one long arm down to me, almost to the ground.
Partway up, the limb opened like a womb
or a wound, a gash big enough for me
to sit in and be things: an aviatrix
with goggles and a long white scarf,
an orphan mothered by a lioness,
a forlorn child. From there I watched
a tarantula lift its hairy black legs
one by one as it tiptoed
across the bare earth below.

The house, white stucco, rambled,
Spanish style, with only one bedroom but
little dressing rooms and a four-bed
sleeping porch where red-headed woodpeckers
tattooed a racket on the tile roof
in the long early morning light.

I was not born to this house, this valley –
they took possession of me later and
possess me still.

THE KETTLE POND

Glacial ice shaped it round
    and deep as a great kettle
        and then disappeared,

to become hill-and-tree locked water,
    a clear round single lens
        waiting to be found.

My mother in silk stockings
    and silly shoes drove us
        in a touring car,

through the oak and pitch pine woods,
    along the sandy ruts,
        to find this secret place.

She spread the picnic hamper
    on its gravel banks: deviled ham,
        little green olives.

The Thermos's cold steel cup
    touched my lips with ice
        and sweet lemonade.

In the tasseled tops of grasses
    at my child's eye level
        a damsel fly hovered

bluer than blue sky or water,
    and hovers still in that child's
        clear round single lens.

A CHILD'S HISTORY OF IRAQ

In the fifth grade, I came to know
the land of Iraq, in its ancient forms:

> Ur of the Chaldees,
> Sumer,
> Assyria and Babylonia,
> the Tigris and Euphrates Rivers,
> the Fertile Crescent lying on the map,
> like a green arc of new moon between
> those rivers and the Mediterranean Sea.

In school, we witnessed the nomadic life of Bedouins
in a grainy black and white film called *Grass*:
We saw children our age herding sheep, watched
while tribesmen pitched wide black tents, built
their cook fires. We followed the graceful strides of
women in their long black embroidered dresses.

Afterwards in the lunchroom I said, *I want to go there,*
I want to live there, and herd sheep and walk
with long strides in a long black embroidered dress
through the dust, under a relentless sun, across low hills
and up dry treeless waddies, but my friends jeered
and raised practical questions. In anger I went home
and wrote stories of my life as a Bedouin, as
an Assyrian princess turned high priestess, as a sheep-
herding boy. I wrote on scraps of paper the size
of ancient clay tablets that fluttered to the floor
around my desk, fragments of the power of images, of words:
Ur of the Chaldees, Sumer, Babylonia and Assyria, the Tigris
and Euphrates Rivers, the Fertile Crescent.

THE SUMMER HOUSE

This hole was the root cellar: in its damp dark
we kept watermelon and blocks of ice, piles of potatoes.
There were little wooden steps and a trap door
my brother threatened to shut on me but never did.

The house stood on stilts in front where the land
fell away to the lake; the back door was ground level.
Here we entered the kitchen where Olga, the local girl,
set fire to the curtains once, though not on purpose.
They hung over the kerosene stove. My mother plunged them
into a pail of water she had made us bring up from the lake.

The chimney still stands – the stones stuck
in cement like door knobs – and the big fireplace
where we warmed ourselves on wet days
and read pulp magazines. Cedar and birch logs
went up like matches, as the house did later.

There, where the chimney rises was the living room,
there the stick desk where I wrote letters
on thin white curls of birch bark. We children climbed
a ladder to the loft to sleep under the wide roof
spread like a great book left open upside down.
Oh, it was hot, sometimes, when we lay down,
but by morning we had pulled up our Hudson's Bays.

The great porch was here, screened against
Canadian mosquitoes, a fierce breed. It looked
over the bay, out to the wild blue lake
darker than sky, clouds floating in it, to islands,
to shoreline of lichen-covered rocks, birch
and pine and cedar. Olga sat on the porch day bed
to sing sad songs to her stringed instrument.

From where that great porch was I see the lake now
through cedar and paper birch and hear the sounds
rising, the drip from canoe paddles, the oarlocks'
chink, boats bumping the dock, girls' voices ringing out –
Lois and Libby, Jean and Joan – we are eleven, twelve,
still girls in underwear tops, unknowing, eager,
exploring far islands by day and dancing half
the lamp-lit night to Paul Whiteman
on a wind-up gramophone.

In late August the air, the lake turned cold.
Skunks and porcupines rustled beneath the house.
In the deep woods a wolf howled, far off.
We packed the car – I wept good-byes – and headed
for our own country. When fire took the house,
we were long gone and did not see it go.

LIBERAL, KANSAS

The train pulls in there early in the morning–
in the Pullman berth, I hear the crossing
bell and raise the green shade.

> The outside world is dim and gray:
>> a sign in an x shape,
>> the lowered gate,
>> a farm truck waiting.

> The street runs straight through the town:
>> square squat houses with chimneys
>> sticking out of pyramidal roofs,
>> trees few and far apart.

Between the dark wood sill and the green shade,
I see a stark world, unadorned,
where another girl leaves her warm bed,
runs across the cold floor, bundles up
to walk the string-straight street to school.

Lying in the lower berth I know this.

> The crossing bell makes a different
> sound as the train pulls out.

III

A WINTER JOURNEY

1. North to Santa Fe

    It grows dark, the road rises, and the sun
    leaves red ribbons on the horizon.
    I drive along the eastern silhouette
    of mountains black and jagged as if ripped
    from the sky's fabric.

    After the last ridge the valley bears
    on its dark blanket an embroidery
    of luminarias, farolitas, a net
    of street lights and blinkers, signs
    of a city, not big, an old city where
    they try to keep the faith.

    I enter this city through tattered
    outskirts and narrowing streets
    that wind toward its heart.

2. August 1935

    One canyon darkened by ponderosa,
    another barren as the badlands,
    the treeless plateau stretching west,
    scrub juniper and piñon scattered
    over tan hills – and dust, half
    Oklahoma blew in – and heat
    the like this child of eastern lakes
    and woodlands had never known:
    They took possession of a deep inner place.

3. A Red-Tailed Hawk

It crosses from one element to another,
from earth to open sky with such ease,
swinging into slow spirals, volutes
and involutes, as it rises higher, higher,
the light passing through the red
tail feathers, the articulated wing tips,
drifting northward to be lost to sight.

I have seen dancers who spread their arms
like those wings and dance with feathers
in their hair and drum like the heartbeats
of all creatures with hearts and stamp
the echoing earth and make the low hums
of wind and water to say:
        We know you are here as we are here.

4. The Hot Springs

In this place many springs
escape from earth, up from deep boiling reservoirs,
through fissures in the rock, remnants of great
geologic movements of fire and magma:
soda springs over 100 degrees, iron springs hotter,
arsenic hotter still.

I go from pool to pool,
in ritual progression when my yearly journey
brings me here: soda-iron-arsenic-iron-soda.
Some years a full moon rises above the sandstone
ridge across the valley; some years it snows,
each flake vanishes on the steaming surface;
this year it is night, moonless with stars
an ancient traveler would bless – Orion, the Pleiades,
Cassiopeia's chair.

Others are here: a workman
soaking his injured back, a woman with arthritic hands,
a couple holding their relaxed bodies close, spirits
of ranchers and farmers who came in wagons, Spaniards
setting aside pantaloons and breastplates, ancient ones
who held these springs sacred. We are quiet, taking in
the place, the night, the heat, the icy air.

My mother introduced me
to hot springs when I was four, she whose womb
gave me my first experience of warm dark waters.
At Wheeler's Hot Springs I dogpaddled across the pool,
and I was happy. Eight decades later I move across
these hot pools, nose and ears just above waterline,
my feet stirring the bottom gravel to release hot bubbles.
Again I am happy.

5. Christmas Eve, Taos Pueblo

When we entered the church, towers
of raw lumber were stacked around
the pueblo's plaza in places
that seemed random but perhaps were not.

When we came out, the night sky
beyond the church door blazed orange
with fire streaked black and smelling
of resin, wind-whipped, howling.

Through the church doorway into this fire
they carried the Virgin Mary
in freshest white on her canopied
litter. She was not afraid,
she who had seen too much.

One hand was raised to bless,
to celebrate, to say all is well:
all suffering ends and begins again.

They carried her among the towers of fire.
Three men led the way, firing old guns
into the air. Then came dancers in animal skins
wearing antlers as headdresses and
scuffing the earth to a drum beat
and the chanting of old men.

We, the crowd, followed, stunned,
bewildered: is God dead or born here?
Which god or gods?

When they brought the Virgin Mary
back to the church, the crowd drifted
away. The fires burned down;
hot ash winked out on the wind,
and night overtook the plaza,
a black night with stars.

6. Christmas Eve, Later

In the bar, drunk, he says,
    I grew up in prison,
and reads his poem that begins
    Me and the rest of them…
The corner fire snaps.
The room holds us like a cave
or a womb or a cell
we can leave at will

7. Christmas Day: Taos Pueblo

In the cold afternoon we waited, a crowd
of a thousand, talking among ourselves,
glancing about, scanning the double and triple
tiers of adobe houses for a sign of a dancer.
Local people lined the flat rooftops, gathered
in doorways, some in jeans and parkas,
others wrapped in bright colored trade blankets
against the cold. They, too, watched and waited.

Near us in the plaza a little group of men began
to chant, one younger than the rest beat a huge drum,

and as if summoned, the dancers appeared, emerging
from the kivas set among the stacked adobes houses.
The antlers appeared first, towering elk headdresses,
the antlered heads of deer, the curved horns of antelope,
the dancers falling in line to cross the stream's
plank bridge, coming toward us where we waited
in the plaza. We pressed back to give them room,
making a great circle.

They entered this circle from the northeast, led in two lines
by two middle-aged women in white embroidered dresses
and tall white moccasin boots, followed by two men,
their naked torsos, their faces smeared white, in white
buckskin and white antlered headdresses. They were
followed by other men, their chests bare, wearing
headdresses of elk, deer, pronghorn, buffalo, the pelts
of wolves and foxes. They held sticks in their hands
and used them like forelegs.

At first, they seemed old men in dramatic costumes
from a lost time and culture, but as they chanted
and beat the drum, the dancers, shuffling their
moccasined feet across the earth, became the animals
and the spirits of animals that had sustained them
for generations. They paid no attention to
the onlookers. They did not dance for us.

8. At Chimayo

    Follow the long mountain road,
a blind poet wrote,
    and you will come to it,

nested in a valley,
protected by wild berry trees.

When you get there, even
blinded, you will know it.
Even the red earth is healing.

9. A Night Chant

I have taken a long road
from distant cities back
to these mountains,
down the ridges of tan earth and piñon,
along dry washes and stream bottoms,
winding toward the great river where
cottonwoods line the banks.
It feels like the right road,
not the only one, but right.

I must have made some kind of offering,
or someone made it for me long ago.

I do not know what it was,
nor where it was done,
nor when, nor who did it.

It may have been done in secret,
perhaps by night.

EAR MOUNTAIN

On top of Ear Mountain, the Blackfeet
cried for a vision, each man alone,
his back against the curved stone wall,
legs straight out in front of him,
crying to the hard empty sky, west
to rising rock walls and scree slopes,
to glacial cirques. Crying east,
to plains of burned grasses, north
where the grizzlies walk and south
across hills of scrub and limber pine.
Crying down, deep into the earth.
Winds blew with a force too great
to stand, cold rain, snow lacerated
his bared body. The fierce sun cracked
his lips, thirsting and hungry, crying.

Then they came, in a delirium of hunger
and thirst and relentless wind:
spirit horses galloped before him;
a buffalo covered him with a robe
from its own shoulders; dead chiefs raised
their feathered pipes to speak only to him.
When they had come and gone, he staggered
down the mountainside to the elders,
men of great power, and only to them
did he repeat the dead chiefs' words.
They listened and gave him food and drink,
a little at a time, and knew his new
spirit name and his purpose, and he
was changed forever.

              I, too, was there,
and not there. I press my ear
to the hard earth, search the empty sky,
plead to gray rock faces and browned prairies
and hills of grass and twisted pine. I cry
to the spirits to come, to tell me my purpose
and bless me with a new name.

BANDELIER

Adolph Francis Alphonse Bandelier, Ethnographer, 1840-1914

When his Indian guide, Juan Jose, said
There is a place where the ancient ones live,
high in the cliffs, he spoke in the present tense.
Bandelier swallowed. *Take me there,* he said.

The road gave out, then the cart tracks. They crossed
the plateau through tall pine and spruce to the point
where the earth ahead split open. They followed
a stream bed lined with aspen and red willow
until the canyon floor widened before them. Juan Jose
led, but some men hung back, muttering prayers
when he pointed up to the dark mouths of caves,
to holes that once held roof beams, to whitened
petroglyphs scratched into the volcanic cliffs.

Bandelier wanted to cry out, *O ancient ones, you are here!*

He made notes and wrote a long letter to his sponsors.
They named the place for him, but it was not his.

MEXICO CITY

She is seven, no more, kneeling on the stone step
of the dry fountain, barefoot in a dirty blue dress.
In front of her is her tea set: tiny pot, two tiny cups,
a plate, her little brother spraddled motionless beside her.

Her father circles the crowd, around his neck a snake
fat as a fire hose, one from the rain forest perhaps
or Yucatan's dry interior. More snakes writhe
in an open box. We stare, motionless as children,
listening to his strange enchantments, watching him
stroke the white throat shingled with scales.

The little girl's lips move. She pours for her brother
and offers him the plate. How comes this street child
to know the niceties of tea: the solicitous politeness,
the careful pouring, the sweet attention, the tiny cup of
refreshment now lifted to her lips?

OAXACA

Early sun stripes the curbside table top.
A sweatered man crosses the zocalo. Stalls
are unshuttered, hung with goods, red
with orange with pink with shades
of green, against the cathedral's pale green
and gold stone. A street singer with guitar
wanders close. *Cafe caliente*, he sings
as I drink mine. A small brown hand
reaches for my toast, a tiny body wrapped
in a rebozo dyed red from insects. I look
into black eyes without irises,
not a child's, an old woman's. *Hambre*,
she whispers, *tengo hambre.*

    In the gray shingled north
    the furnace rouses,
    the snow falls straight down.

PULSE

The dwarf stepped out of the crowd and
     held up his arms to me
     as I was passing
     on the sidewalk
     near Ocho Rios Bay.

Did he want me to pick him up,
     hold him, against my shoulder?
     But he was a grown man,
     middle-aged, smiling.

I held out my arms to him,
     he took my hands,
     and then we were dancing
     together in the street.

Someone in the crowd thumped a bongo,
     and we both laughed
     and turned, and he
     twirled under my arm –
     his little feet sliding over
     the pavement – and we danced
     passing, turning, spinning

The bongo slowed and
     he let me go, first one hand,
     then the other, hesitating
     on the beat, and we separated,
     smiling, as if we knew each other,
     in the darkening Jamaican street.

IV

BLUE BONES

He pulled the fish in
   from sapphire waters
      off the black sand beach.

It was so long and skinny
   we took it for an eel
      with fins and forked tail.

It's good eating, the cook said,
   as he coiled the long
      body in the skillet.

When he brought it to us, the flesh
   was falling off the bones,
      and the bones were blue.

They turn blue when they're cooked,
   the cook said, and they were
      sapphire as the waters

the fish left behind. Then
   we fell on the sweet flesh,
      two cannibals devouring

an enemy's brave spirit,
   certain of the magic that
      turns bones sapphire blue.

FLY CASTING

He stepped into the Snake River
    in jeans and tennis shoes,
his fish rod held high. From the bank
    I saw him slip, catch himself,
before his next step into the current.
    The icy river lapped his hips.

If you slip, I can't save you,
    I cried from the bank.
    He grinned and waved.

If he slipped, he would rise
    in a day or two, belly up
like a great German brown trout
    caught under a cottonwood branch,
below willow thickets webbed with fly line,

    beneath the great mountains –
    Moran, the Grand Teton –
    pocked with glaciers,
    serrating the sky.

He wades toward the dark mountains
    casting as he goes,
his rod whipping forward, backward, forward,
    the line in figure-eight loops.

The fly touches the water
    and drifts for an instant on the current.

THE CREMATORY

I stand behind the velvet rope,
alone and not alone,
in the back room
where the ovens are.
Men in green work clothes
bring in his body
in a cardboard box like long-stemmed roses.
They place it on the conveyor
that moves it slowly through steel doors
into the fire.

Outside the August sun
is a copper disk stuck
in a pewter sky. The road
hot as fire leads away
to some new place I do not know.
I get lost on my way home.

ON THE SNAKE RIVER

the white pelican

alone

where the river

bends

why

must summer

end

ON NECESSITY STREET

1998-2003

I

ON NECESSITY STREET

There is inner, and there is outer, dear Ramon, I said,
as we strolled along the park's pathway.

　　　　　　　　　　　　And the imagined, he said.

I wore my long gray coat with the matching feather
collar that he likes.

　　　　　　　Ramon is shorter than I am, a little stout
these days, and walks with a cane and an appealing limp.

　　　　　　　　　　　　　　Why, he
asked me once, *don't you color your hair, henna perhaps?*

And I replied, *Because I liken myself to Kilimanjaro, crowned with snow.*

　　　　I should have guessed, he said.

　　　　　　　　　　　　The snow fell gently,
thickly. Joggers passed, mouths open to the flakes, power
walkers pumping their arms.

　　　　　　　　*Perhaps I should get a turquoise
running suit and white ploppy shoes to go with it.*

　　　　　　　　　　　　And he said,
But we know ourselves by our differences.

　　　　　　　　　　　True, I said,
but still, turquoise silk…

With a matching turban, Ramon said,
and a peacock feather in front.

*I'd lose myself as
Kilimanjaro. I would have to reinvent.*

You can do it, he
said and went on, *Did you know the brain uses the same
neurons when you imagine a thing as when you look at
that thing?*

*You mean, when I think of you and when I see you,
it is the same?*

And he said, *To the neurons, it seems, yes.*

Well! I said, *I never would have guessed.*

We scuffed the snow,
leaving long prints, holes where his cane tapped.

*I had a dream
last night*, I said. *I was looking for a friend, but I could not
remember her address. Then I found it – she lived on Necessity
Street.*

An important street, he said, *an important dream.*

It may have been Necessary Street, I said.

Even more
important, he said, and we laughed.

I took his arm. *Ah, Ramon,*
forget the neurons. I prefer you in person.

And we went back to my place at a leisurely pace.

II

THE ICE FOREST

It happened overnight:
rain drenched the winter world,
the temperature fell, and I awoke
in a forest of ice – outside my windows
every twig and needle, every blade
and branch encased in ice; wires hung
with icicles from pole to house to pole;
the hoods of birdfeeders fringed like lampshades;
blue spruce iced to perfection; tall
white pines frozen against a rain-dark sky.

At the center of this world I went
from window to window, room to room,
a willing prisoner surrounded by such beauty
only a mad ice sculptor would envision,
or Adams see, holding up the wet film of a world
where light is dark, black is white,
and everything, glistening, is right.

FROM A WINTER NIGHT

Through the layers –
      blankets, down comforter –
the distant rumbling of the snow plow,
      the sand truck following.
Oh, the sweet pleasure of burrowing deeper.

A midnight high moon
      lacing the snow
with skinny black shadows
      from tall bare trees,
the air like ice in the nose.

      I remember walking a dog
         to Schlosser's grocery store
      in Winnetka on Elm Street
         on the east side of the tracks.
      It had fragrant sawdust on the floor.

Why do I think of this
      seventy years later
in the middle of a winter night?

      It wasn't my dog.

SPRING: NEW ENGLAND

This is the snow that turned to water.
This is the rain that melted the snow.
These are the snow banks that channeled the road.
This is the driveway that was also so.
This the garage the water flooded
Over the hubcaps of two silent cars.

This is the threshold the flood waters entered.
This is the basement without a drain.
These are the books that stood on the floor.
These the papers of a writing household.
These are the letters from World War II.
These the snapshots of everything since.

This is the heap of sodden cardboard.
This the stink of devouring mildew.
This the maché of irretrievable words.

Now comes the sun, the clear blue skies.
Now the disclaimer of cause and effect.

LATE SPRING

Magnolia
weeping Korean cherry
three kinds of daffodils
red maple tassels carpeting the blacktop
ornamental pear in bridal white
yellow-green weeping willow
red buds edging every red bud branch
bluets and violets in the grass
outsized green skunk cabbage
in shrinking vernal pools
all of them
at once
in this brief, sense-flooded now

THE MAILBOX

Among the silver barked beeches on the corner,
in the grove that shimmers yellow in the fall
and keeps its dry tan leaves all winter,
there is one beech with a mail box deep in its trunk.

Years – years back – someone nailed it to the silver bark,
and it did its job – receiving bills, Christmas cards,
tax statements, summons to jury duty, letting its maw
be stuffed with unwanted catalogs and seductive
flyers to hike the Dolomites or cruise Antarctica,
a diminishing number of personal letters.

Nailed to a tree it resisted Saturday night teenagers
with baseball bats, parents returning late from
a party. It was well placed to survive until
it began to disappear, enfolded by the same
pale gray trunk that saved it.

Each year, I noticed it recede. The mouth
lost its cover, the supports rusted, the side walls
crumpled. Once I reached inside to the very back.
The metal plate had gone, and I could feel
the damp wood hidden in its darkest, innermost
place where heart wood, tree rings lie.
I pulled my hand back as if I had touched
the forbidden, the sacred, the feel of time itself.

Now all you can see is the crushed maw where
the catalogs were stuffed, an elbow of the twisted
supports. In a year or two it will be gone.
The beech will have enfolded it, taken it into itself.
There will be no outward trace on the silver bark.

ENDANGERED

In the cut grass behind a cottage in upstate
New York I saw a stone move, but not a stone,
a just-born turtle the size of a small stone,
its dark still-soft shell imprinted with its life,
its head extended, tiny splay-toed forefeet
pushing aside green blades, little pointed tail
between its legs. I've seen a newborn turtle
before, a miniature sea turtle, paddling hard
across a hot Jamaican beach, it, too, alone.

I hold this one in my hand – it's smaller
than my palm. It arches its neck,
tests the air with one forefoot, prepares
to withdraw. I set it down and wish it well.

After that, two cinnamon fawns studied me
as they drank; a chipmunk half-left the safety
of his hole to watch me; a hummingbird sat still
in the trumpet vine above my head:

Could they know through sight or scent or sense
something about me that I hardly know myself?

IN MINIATURE

I saw the tail first, dangling
from the edge of the green umbrella,
a black segmented tail as thin as wire
hung in a graceful downward arc.

It belonged to the smallest of dragonflies
that rested on the umbrella's edge and
had spread out its oval coppery wings,
the October sun illuminating
its delicate and intricate veins,

its body not a body but
a tiny tube, its legs folded on
themselves like paper clips,
the head a black hat pin with antennae
reaching out to test the air.

It rubbed its black forelegs together
without a sound, not one I could hear,
lifted its tail over its back like
a construction crane with work to do.
Then the tail curved downward,
the end slowly coiling in a tight spiral.

The next instant on the strength of legs alone
it rose in the air, hesitated and was gone,
leaving the empty air imprinted with its elegance.

III

WALKING STICKS

In the spring of the year
the cambium is so wet with sap
any old pocket knife will strip
the bark in one long sweep.

All the old codgers knew this,
whittling on their Adirondack porches
in plaid mackinaws and grimed caps,
smelling the sweet maple, feeling it
wet as a newborn and yellow white
like cream clotted in milk bottle necks.

My Lady Bug knife slips
under the soft bark, bares
the pale wood in long strips.
I whittle. No purpose,
no chair or bench in mind,
until one stick stands on three legs
and leans like a naked human into the wind.

I bare another, then another, until
there are six, seven, eight, a small crowd
of stick figures, each one pale, stripped
and skinny, leaning intently forward,
walking somewhere, not knowing where.

BURYING GROUND

Red cedar, swamp maple, black locust populate
what were fields clear cut for crops
and pasture not so long ago. Not a trunk
was left standing in those days, other than
this oak, an oak now fifteen feet in girth,
fifty in reach, more in height. I found it
in the rain, walking up from the river
through my neighbor's woods. In the old days
one oak was often left, the farmer's oak,
a custom centuries old when it came here
buried in some farmer's Druidic heart.

I found the fallen grave stones beneath the oak,
slate slabs dark with age and rain, names and winged
death's heads erased. Who lies – or lay – here
in white pine boxes or a furl of sail rotted long
since. Mrs. Turner's progeny, perhaps. It's in
the deed to our land to let her cross it to the sea
with her team and wagon. When we hear strange night
noises, my husband says, *There goes Mrs. Turner*.

I see little graveyards tucked in corners of all
the old farms. Someone tends them, mows around
the slant-wise slabs, weed-whacks the edges. One
is at the high school next to the playing fields.
The stones wear scabs of green and ochre lichens
and names and dates: *Sofia Peckham Aged 84 Yrs,
Deacon Benjamin Tripp b. 1774* and other Tripps
laid out in several rows. No one knows about
the graves under the farmer's oak.

More than people have died in this town. There were
working dairy farms on our road when we came here,
and a store-post office, a place to ask questions
and hear gossip, gone now, swept away by a wind
as murderous as the hurricane of 1938.

There is no graveyard corner on our land. Perhaps
we should start one: seven slate slabs for seven
dairy farms, one for the store-post office,
one for our wine grape vineyard lost to disease
and reluctance to spray, and one for Mrs. Turner,
her team and wagon. We will have to plant a farmer's oak.

BATTLEGROUND

Stones rise up out of these fields like turnips
every time a plow rips the black soil into ridges,
and you give them half a chance.

Stones have a life of their own, and I mean life.
Those who say they are inert don't know stones
or earth, either. Dropped here the last time
glaciers melted, when the mother ice
left them behind, they have lived under this
blanket of black earth, waiting their turn,
biding their time like slaves or serfs
that outnumber their masters.

Years back, we plowed every spring. Each time,
the stones rose up, every size and shape
granite can take: cannon balls, boulders, Cyclopean
slabs, ten sizes of gravel pressed hard into pudding stones.
Each time, we picked rocks out of the wild chamomile
and daisies that sprang up around them
in the disturbed earth.

One spring, we looked at each other, slow
learners, and let the fields go back to grass.
We knew why ancestral folk left these farms
behind, with their stone walls and stone-
lined cellar holes and stone chimneys and
stone-marked family graveyards. Ohio, Iowa,
even Nebraska looked good. Eventually,
you know it when you're outnumbered.

THE BUFFALO

Twilight edges the rounded hills
and the great rounded black-brown backs
as the buffalo drop their heads
to crop tufted grasses
and yellow sweet clover.

A great horned black bull
moves in our direction, lifting
his heavy head, flexing his robed
shoulders, shivering his flanks.
He comes close, and we see deep
into his black eyes to days and nights
on this prairie when it was his alone.

In the dusk the herd begins to move
across the hillside. Cows, bulls, playful
calves, we hear them calling
among themselves, soft, secret sounds
that drift toward us across
a sea of time and grass.

TWO TREES

1. Limber Pine

Winds you can't stand up to
sweep these prairies. I see them now
in the shapes of limber pine spun like tops,
twisted, leaning away, whipped to the core,
the skeletons white as limestone among
the tanned grasses. Prairie bones, they speak
to the dry hollow wind as does the falcon
hanging black in the wind-streaked sky.

2. The Hanging Tree

Among trees, cottonwoods have their own place.
For height, for girth, they rival oaks, maples, beeches.
The bark's thickness, its deep cracks and fissures, are its
own. In arid country, they give greenness, shade along

unwinding western rivers as they cross the plains,
the Yellowstone, the Missouri, the Rio Grande,
the Chama. It's not a long-lived tree, fifty years,
more or less, before its great bulk falls.

This cottonwood stands at the mouth of a box canyon.
Years back, the canyon made a cattle rustlers' hide-out,
the tree the end for the hapless cowboy who
came looking for the stolen herd.

Early one spring morning, I looked up to see
the hanging tree spread-eagled against storm clouds,
itself hung, a sky-borne crucifix.

Every new green leaf, every limb caught the
first light, its huge bulk, its strength laid bare
for a moment revealing everything but the mystery of
the men who did the deed and the man done in.

IV

THE FOUNDRYMAN

It took half the day to melt the scrap –
old radiators, rusting steel, ingots of iron,
you name it – all day before it reached
twenty-five hundred, the right heat,
all day for the men to form the molds
in rows on each side of the main aisle.

Then the bung was drawn, and white hot metal
flowed into the bull ladle. Emil steadied it
as it swung on ways up the aisle. They met it
with hand ladles. Some wore gloves,
goggles maybe, steel toes in their shoes.
Emil and Garner poured, and Moony Garrow,
Vasily, a double row of them, they filled
the molds for pitcher spout pumps, handles,
pipe, four-way connections.

Moony held rock-steady as he poured. He didn't lose
a drop. He was the best, and they knew it.
They saw his pay check at Tiedeman's on
Friday night, more for quantity, more
for quality. They gave him bullshit,
but they knew. That's what they did
in those days. That was work.

FOR THE LOVE OF BRIDGES

For the love of bridges:
      the wood beams and dried out planks
      that span a creek in red rock country,
      the wilderness rope walkway swinging
      high above the Flathead's South Fork,
      the rusted iron skeleton of a bridge
      across the frozen Wapsipinnicon,
      the workaday flat concrete deck
      that carries the interstate across
      the Mississippi River into Iowa cornfields,
      the mile long line of steel arches
      looping over tidal New Jersey marshes,
      the stone arch bridge deep in Weetamoo Woods,
      Padanaram harbor's little draw bridge
      rising on a summer evening to let
      sailors come home from the sea.

For love of the great bridges:
      the long curved stretch of the Golden
      Gate's red cables, its red steel towers,
      the uncoiling concrete curve
      high above San Diego bay and
      the Brooklyn, oh, the Brooklyn –
      bridge of bridges – with its rough stones,
      its Gothic arches, its cables in
      infinite numbers – photographed,
      painted, sung in memorable verse.

For the love of bridges:
        I waited with thousands of others (most
        behind me) to walk a new bridge,
        one with slender gray piers
        like wish-bones upside down, with
        cable covers white as seagulls' wings
        fanning out from each column.
        It rained as we walked and a band
        played, trumpets and noses dripping,
        but oh, it was a glorious day for
        bridge lovers to be there, to walk there, to see
        this delicate white and gray span, its
        soaring elegance and be close enough to touch.

THE GOOD TIMES CAFÉ

I go in, hungry, hesitant,
and it's dim, a juke box lit red,
playing big band, posters all around:
Lombard, Gable, *The Thin Man,*
a real soda fountain with a dummy
soda jerk by the door in a white cocked hat –

it's like high school 1938 –
there's Al behind the counter –
he had a cauliflower ear.

The waitress, sweet, blank young thing,
asks for my order, and I say,

Grilled American cheese on white
with a fountain Coke.

There wasn't anything else.

ON THE BEACH

The light comes and goes
through breaks in the rain
The tide laps the sand with the sound
of a cat drinking from the far side of its bowl.

The sand is coarse and goes to pea gravel
and larger – rough under foot.
I find a stone marked with yin and yang
and another rolled like a sticky bun.

I pass a boy playing catch with a man,
the boy's legs in braces.
His right hand sprouts from his elbow.
He throws left-handed, and when the man misses,
the boy shouts and twirls his elbow hand like a pinwheel.

What's your name? the man, asks.
Peter, the boy says. The man misses.
I'll call you Pedro. The boy shouts
and spins his hand limp as a rubber glove.

I leave them behind in the rain
and search the sand for bits of beach glass –
finding green chips from last year's beer bottles,
a piece milky white, smooth, older.

When I return, boy and man are gone. I wait
for a motionless blue heron standing
in the tidal shallows,
for the foghorn's next lowing,
for the voice deeply remembered,
no longer heard.

THE BLUE CRAB

The blue crab's long claws embrace
a funereal mound of seaweed.

Eyes in blue eye sockets, blue bumps
along what may be a spine,

the underside armored in scallops,
and the tail tucked into its slot.

The long blue-knuckled legs dangle lifelessly.
Only the deadly fore claws are recognizably blue,

the beak like a small bird's, unmoving.
Death carries its own perfection.

RAGS OF TIME

2003-2010

I

A BOOK OF HOURS

MATINS

They stalk this house at 4 a.m.
Heels click on stone, then stop, a knock,
planks shift. Is it the fridge that starts?
The heels again. I know them well,
these monsters of the still dark hour:
the guilt and shame, regrets and terrors.
My heart bangs, my sweat chills the sheet.
Help me forget these long-past errors.
Lay fear to rest and let me sleep.

LAUDS

The world holds still, silent, beneath
a sky the palest pewter. A wind
sweeps the trees and lifts the heavy limbs.
A few leaves glitter gold. And then
our fiery star rises to view
above the hill. Now night is over,
and life returns, revives, renews,
all glorious because it is,
this daily resurrection.

PRIME

Now is the hour for lists, the day's
docket, for ordering of deeds,
words, thoughts, a time for friends, the earth,
the long walk on the beach or through
the reddened oaks. Was it always so?

To call this hour prime speaks to lost
and ancient wisdoms only found
within walled monasteries where
they knew them well and feared worldly
pride, idleness, sloth, anger, lust,
and cried for help to reach day's end
with conscience by the world unstained.

TERCE

These are the little hours that go
unmarked in daily time. I am
on my own to improvise a way
to keep my head and heart in line.

SEXT

In all things visible there lies
a hidden wholeness, so Merton
said, and here at noon when all
shadows are foreshortened and we
are struck by light as unconditional
as life, I ask for power to see
this wholeness, the workman in the work,
the garden in the gardener.

NONE

The red heads of bergamot and spikes
of lavender are bouncing
with autumn bees. The herbal fragrance
fills this arched and cloistered walk.
I hear my sisters' voices ring
like bells on ancient stones worn down
by many feet as calloused as mine
and by many hems as dusty.

EVENSONG

Now this day is over and the night
waits just beyond the horizon
flaming with the sun's final hour.
What prescience, after the bang, to set
a daily round of light and dark,
of warmth and coolness, work and rest!
These hearts and voices fill with thanks.
Surely, this, this is to be blessed.

COMPLINE

Alone in darkness I will say
my gratitude for this one day
and hope that I discharged the debt
I owe for this most valued gift.

II

THE ABYSS

Once, in a dream,
    I came to an abyss
    that I had to cross with only
    a slender rope to walk on.

I halted. Another woman appeared
    who ran across the abyss,
    without a glance
    into the dark below.

Without thinking I followed, and halfway
    across I began to laugh.
    It was so easy!
    I woke up laughing.

Now, in this dream,
    I walk the edge of an abyss, the stone rim
    dusted with quicklime, below, a tumble of bodies
    like a mass grave in some ravaged country.

Is this the same abyss?

    I can't find the rope.

THE RAT CODEX a fragment

*In this clay figure, a man is transformed into his
way, or supernatural other, a guardian animal*
Label, Boston Museum of Fine Arts

1

After the war, in my captivity, I did not fully recover
from my wounds. My legs are bowed where they were
broken by blows of the stone ax. One ear is half gone.
Nonetheless, I came to manage the king's farms, to decide
what should be planted, how the water ditches should be
dug, how the dry storage houses for corn and grains should
be built, and the cool cellars for potatoes and round
smooth squashes. I became known for my competence,
my honesty, my foretelling, and my access to the king.

I served the king for three years before Rat came.
An illness left me longing for my own people, my own
language, my own fields and mountains. *We will go
there*, Rat said, *Get the small pipe and tobacco*.
I smoked until I felt the swelling between my shoulders,
up the back of my neck, my nose changing until he and I
were one. Then he carried me through undulating colors,
through darkness to the unlit fields and mountains and
villages of my home country. I saw the people destitute
and knew what they needed and how to help them.
When we returned, I presented a plan to the king – it was
much to his benefit, and he smiled and said, *Do it*.
That year my people prospered. They gave fewer in slaves
as their fields yielded more in tribute. The king honored me
for this.

Afterwards, his favored woman took me aside to
give me her approval. She rested her hand on
my arm and whispered, *Come to me tonight*.

But, madam, I cannot, I said.

Her eyes flashed, *Come to me. Tonight.*

When the king demanded, his warriors gave him
their women. Later, when their breasts and bellies
swelled, it was an honor to their lineage, they said.
The king had beautiful women of his own, some
acquired in war, some by agreement. Because I
was a slave, of small stature, crippled, and close
to the king, they spoke to me. They asked me
to speak to the king of their needs for jewels,
robes, a slave, a child, each wanting more
than the others, something more than the woman
the king favored. This woman – I dare not say her name –
often took me aside to give me words of advice for the
king. *But madam,* I said, *you can speak yourself.*

You are a man, she would say.

Within me, I felt Rat stir warily, and I trembled.

Do not fear, Rat said.

That night, I lay on my pallet in the king's chambers
and whispered, *Rat, Rat, what do I do?* Rat did not
reply. I felt the swelling between my shoulders, in my neck,
my face changing to a long nose, a lop-sided ear.
He and I scampered on silent rat feet through
the chambers, not opening doors. One watchman
kicked at us, but we were too quick for him.

We slipped along the night-dark walls until we entered

the private quarters of this favored woman. There, Rat
left me, saying he would return before light. I lay beside
her beneath a feathered robe and gave myself to her
again and again. When she slept, Rat returned and he
and I ran through the silent chambers to the king's
apartment. He was calling for his morning gourd.

I knew it was the beginning of the end. I had betrayed
my lord benefactor to save my own heart. If his favored woman
demanded again, I would have to go to
save it again, to enjoy the great transports of our bodies.
If her belly swelled and she gave birth to a boy-child
of small stature with bandy legs, would the king take it
as an honor to his lineage? *Rat*, I whispered, *save me.*

The next day the king called me to his audience hall,
and I went, shaking with fear, the sweat pouring down
my cheeks.

Are you ill? he asked.

A small fever, I said, my voice scraping my throat. *It will
pass.*

They are restive in the far lands I have newly conquered,
he said. *Go there. Make them content. I will send warriors
with you.*

As the next sun rose, I was on my way accompanied by
five warriors, and three slaves bearing our necessities.

Rat, I whispered, *is this your doing?* Rat did not reply.

We crossed mountains and followed game trails
through dense forest for five days until suddenly
the forest opened onto a great stretch of sand
and an endless expanse of sea. It was a land of
incomparable beauty, but there were no houses,
no temples, no fields, and the sands were deserted.
No people moved about, tending fires, no women
pounding cassava into meal. The fires were dead.
I kicked through the coals and burnt logs of one, thinking,
these restive people have fled, but why would they flee
from a band of nine men. Then I saw, among the burnt
logs charred bones, and picked one up. It was a human
bone, the lower leg. *These people eat men,* I said to a
warrior. He grunted. We went to other fire pits. They were
the same. *They will appear,* I said, *when they see our
small number.* One of the slaves caught a turtle which we
cooked, and another found a cache of corn beer. We
took over a thatched hut and ate and drank. I fell asleep
wondering where these restive people had gone.

When I awoke, the sun was full in my eyes. I stretched but
my arms would not move, my legs were heavy, my head
pounded. I spoke to the warrior beside me, but he was
not there. I called out once. There was no reply. I listened,
but I heard no one stirring. I looked at my arms and legs –
they were bound to stakes in the ground. The sand
was hard as a well-traveled road beneath the thatch.
Then I heard someone stirring a fire, smelled the first smoke,
heard a voice in a strange language. A shadow came
between me and the sun. Men stared at me and spoke to
each other. Then they went away.

I lay back and whispered, *Rat – Rat, save me.*

2

The first time, it knocked me flat,
landing on my back and wrapping
its huge white wings around
my shoulders. They are strong,
believe me. The white feathers brushed
my chin. I lay quietly, feeling
its heart beat in the mighty chest
as it fused with mine, feeling
my arms become wings, and its-our
breath begin to rasp in the deadly beak.
In a moment, we soared above the earth.

MIRIAM'S SONG

       I showed Pharaoh's daughter where
my brother lay. At six, I did as I was told. Even so,
they listened and followed. I walked with a staff
at ten. I was taller than most, my skirts swung
with my long stride. In the market a tar-black woman
cried, *Prophetess,* when she saw me
and bowed deep. She tied the little clay bells
to my staff so they would hear me as I came.
I knew her from long ago, from another life.
Later I tied goatskin sacks for potions and herbs.

       At thirteen, I lay with a camel driver,
and he taught me to tell the future. On the beach
at night, sailors from across the sea showed me
the stars, told me the waters rose and fell with the moon
in some places. Men do not lie to me,
fearing a curse. The first time I fell and thrashed
the earth, people stared. I saw their fear, and then
I knew my calling.

       All the while, my brothers,
Moses and Aaron, lived at court where sorcerers
taught them the tricks: how to make things appear,
to turn a rod into a serpent, to make it
bloom. They were quick studies. Aaron, I loved.
Bitter, Moses cried for attention and grew up
prideful and arrogant with his women
and his murderous rages. He had to flee.

After the firstborn were murdered,
and outrage seethed, I sought Moses in the desert.
That night, I beckoned him to me.
We must go to a new place, I told him,
beyond the reddened sea. I knew. My bones
ached and pulled me eastward.
But how? Everyone? he cried. *They have horses,*
chariots, their spear throwers I've watched.
Everyone! I said. *Follow me.*

      I gathered all our people,
saying I had seen the future and worse
was in store for us. They hung back, reluctant
to leave what they knew, but they came.
We set out by moonlight, each with a burden.

      I led the way,
heading the column. Aaron followed.
Moses – he strode along beside the wives.
We were in sight of the sea when we heard them
coming to trap us between the sea and their swords.
Moses came on the run, crying *What will we do?*
I was at the water's edge. *Be quick,* I said.
The moon is full. The sea has been drawn away
but will return. We must go forward now.
He went back along the line urging them
onward, letting me go first.

I was afraid,
but I strode into the sea. The waters lapped my neck,
my chin, my ears. We struggled all night.
I dared not stop. By early light, I saw
the other shore. Cheers rang along the column.
We were on dry sand. *We're free, we're free!*
The water rose again and swept away
the horsemen and chariots and spear throwers.
We slew easily those who came across and lost
only a few of our own.

My skirts dried
in the morning sun. At the water's edge I sang,
Sing to the creator who has triumphed gloriously!
That night we built a fire, and we danced
and sang, *Sing to the creator who has triumphed.*
But Moses jumped on a rock and cried, *We sing
to the Lord for he has triumphed gloriously.*
They turned to him as to their master.

After that,
Moses turned from me and forsook my counsel.
Shunned Aaron, too.

When the itching dryness
covered my body, oh, I saw the future then.

PILGRIMS
(Japan, 1690)

My father's house stands where two roads cross:
one, north-south, is rutted by market carts;
the other leads pilgrims to temples by the sea.

The pilgrims know there is always a bowl
of noodles and broth in my father's house and
stand their sticks and bundles by the plank door.

Clogs in a row, they bow and greet him, kneel
at table, their cold hands around hot mugs
of tea, their aches diminishing bit by bit.

When my mother and sister bring bowls of noodles,
they slurp them hungrily, crying approval.
Then saké in long-necked bottles.

From childhood my father allowed me to sit
with them and listen, to learn of the world
and other things, the making of poems.

For years I listened to pilgrims turn that day's
journey, sore feet, budding willow, into verse,
also anger into forgiveness.

The great Bashō came when I was nine.
Between sips of saké he spoke three lines,
then cried, *The boy, let him speak.*
I squeaked and stammered,
    What can the shoot say
    to the full-grown banana tree?

Bashō and his companion struck their hands
and laughed, and he spoke again three lines
and I replied with two more that sprang to my lips.

After that my father included me in the circle
as the verse traveled round the table,
each of us adding our brief lines.

A great lady with her entourage came
just to hear me, a woman so beautiful
in robes so fine my sister spilled the tea.

The day I turned fourteen, a great man appeared,
alone, his robe wet under his straw rain cape.
As I took his clogs, I felt his power.

At table his verse heated my blood and sent it
racing. I sipped a little saké –
it was my birthday – before giving mine.

That night my sister went to him. I heard
her delighted cries. And afterward
I went to him also. How can I forget him?

In this way I learned the high arts of words,
of love, of food and generosity, without
ever leaving my father's crossroads house.

Spring rain, autumn wind,
a pilgrim travels farthest through
the fires in his heart.

III

ON MY 77th BIRTHDAY

In the snapshot
my brother sent
I recognize the place, the bunch grass,
the gravelly earth, the distant outline
of Mingus Mountain
like a thrown steer,

And I recognize the horse,
black rump, black chest,
white blaze down her nose,
one white foreleg lifted to run.

It's the rider I don't recognize, the girl,
her hair blowing in the wind
like the horse's mane,
boots, jeans, an old shirt,
sitting so easily in the saddle.

Can it be me?
Before it all happened?

She is looking straight at me,
sixty years her senior.
What can I say to her?
There were reasons, conditions,
things happen, I can explain,
and it came out all right.

But she isn't really asking
or listening.

AFTER SEPTEMBER 11, 2001
IN MEMORIAM: the three thousand, the twin towers

I walk these days in healing places:

I walk the path around a small New England lake
shaded by great oaks and white pines, take
notice of the calm waters, greener where
water lilies lie, where a white gull floats.

In this season of mellow fruitfulness and gentle decline,
in slanted September light I walk in the shadow of death
and fear evil, the evil done to us, the evil we do in return.

December 7, 1941:

After Quaker meeting that Sunday, after dinner,
the news had broken: Pearl Harbor bombed.
Pearl Harbor? Where is that? Hawaii? No one
had been there. We wandered from dorm room
to dorm room. We saw the pictures later, but
we knew: our futures joined in a dark collective destiny.

August 6, 1945:

In the shadow of the Wabash Avenue elevated
I read the headline, *Atomic Bomb Dropped
on Japan*. I went to the next newsstand
and read again, frightened, jubilant.

I walk the perimeter of Walden Pond, sacred
spring-fed lake, stop at the foundation of
Thoreau's house and drop my stone on the heaped cairn.
A maple has turned to flame.

    September 11, 2001:

    I am become death, shatterer of worlds.

I walk a long Atlantic beach, the tide far out,
hard sand under foot. Sandpipers skitter
ahead of me, a flight of blackbirds passes
overhead, wings catching the light as they
wheel southward across a pathless sea.

SEPTEMBER 28, 2001

...into the light of common day.
Wordsworth, *Intimations of Immortality*

Each day, each sunrise
in a newly flushed sky,
each sunset red with polluted haze,
each moonrise, the brief brilliance
of evening stars, Orion's
climb up the early morning sky
with his huddled companion Pleiedes,
the hum of school bus tires on
the early morning road,
a leaf blower next door at 7 a.m. –
these common things, these things
we hold in common
on any given common day.

ON TURNING 80

Don't be too eager to ask
What the gods have in mind for us.
Horace, *Ode i.11* (translated by David Ferry)

On the richest chocolate cake
the numbers,
the smooth roundness of them,
the stacked double 0 of the 8
followed by the singleton 0,
circles of completion that
bring counting to a close.

Enough! Let the 8-0 stand
as gateway, marking where
the paved road ended,
where the road bed became ruts
washed out in flash floods,
potholes everywhere.

It gets dark much earlier now.
The time we have is short.
Horace again, *Seize the day.*
Is there light enough to play?

AN OCTOGENARIAN CONSIDERS FORGIVENESS

The stone steps downward
through the little amphitheater,
the half-rings of seats filled
with flowered chiffon and garden party hats,

me in my pink crepe de chine dress
hand smocked, a little basket of rose petals
on my arm – I scattered some on each step.

The other flower girl didn't strew her rose petals.
She didn't stay on her side.
She clung to me, weepy and fearful.

What was her name?
May – Mary – Ma – Malou – yes,
Malou Ger – Ger – maybe Gerard –

I gave her a shove.
She stayed on her side after that.

OCTOBER 31, 2005

A breath-taking near-death experience
David Ferry, *On Turning Eighty*

A heavenly day: 70 degrees, mostly sunny,
breeze WSW, my 84th birthday,

And fall color at last all at once:
russet oaks beside red and gold maples
beside beeches almost pumpkin yellow,
leaves reddening on wild blueberry,
burning bush just catching fire.

I take myself to Walden Pond, to walk around it,
my birthday ritual: people are out in canoes, rafts,
swimming, fly-casting, sunning themselves,
one old man wading like a five year old, shoes in hand.

I hike the sunny north bank to Thoreau's cabin –
or where it once was – and leave a stone on the cairn
first begun in 1872, sit on a rock to eat a crisp apple.

I circle the pond, returning on the shadowed
chill south bank, climb the steep steps to the road –
breathless by the time I make the top – and find
myself one glorious hour closer to my demise.

AN OCTOGENARIAN CONTEMPLATES BEING ONE

Is there a point to all this longevity?
And if there is a point,
        what is it?

MY EIGHTY-FIFTH WALTZ

What did you say?
Were you speaking to me?

You said eighty-five?

You said eighty-fifth?

How is this possible?
Can you mean me?

But it can't be – I don't feel eighty-five –
not that I know what it feels like to be...

Who's there to tell me?
Not many women, hardly a man.

Mirror, mirror on the wall,
is that really me I see?

and if it's so, tell me then,
what does me really mean?

Here I go round again,
round again
round again

Here I go round again,
how can this be?

AN OCTOGENARIAN THINKS OF HER FUTURE

As I am carried aloft on invisible wings:

Will I see again the webbed lights of Boston,
Chicago, Nogales, Billings, Montana?

Will I see again maples redden, oaks turn brown, birches
yellow, wineberries ripen in hedgerow brambles?

Will I see again glacial rivers sweeping
around red granite cliffs? Will I soak again
in springs heated deep in the earth?

Will I see the night sky and its strew of stars,
planets, constellations, meteors and
meteorites, a hundred thousand galaxies?

Will I see double rainbows across the heavens?

Will I know him again? Will he know me?

Will I watch again the sun touch the snow-pocked Tetons,
slide down their eastern slopes to light the prairie
carpets of yellow sweet clover?

Will I hear trumpets and trombones, French
horns and tubas, Berlioz in Dixieland,
the viola in Beethoven's late-life quartet?

Will I hear the cadences of Shakespeare's
Fear No More when I need to hear them?

Will I meet troops of friends on the road,
battered, wounded, helping each other along,
looking like a Civil War retreat?

Will I remember the pain?

Will I feel gratitude for a full life, darkened
by its sorrows?

Just once more will I see a hawk floating over
eight lanes of traffic, wings outstretched,
every feathered tip etched against the sky?

AN OCTOGENERIAN BROWSES THE NEW TALBOTS CATALOG, LOOKING FOR FLANNEL PAJAMAS

Cover shock: a high fashion model in skin-tight top and pants,
one arm flung wide, legs crossed in a tango step, more like
Suzy Parker in an Avedon photo than Talbots.

Not my age group but surely inside…

But inside more of same: skinny women in skinny dresses,
long legs in skin-tight jeans, lush heads of hair, none gray,
blank faces a mortician would die for, mouths ajar,
beautiful of course, wearing enough costume jewelry
to sink a yacht.

Do they want me to buy something and if so what?

They have hired a celebrity stylist and a Chief Creative Officer –
Has war been declared and if so who is the enemy?

I fear it is me.

On page 32 I see a nice silk shirt, long sleeves, camp shirt pockets –
I could wear that
On page 39 a ruffled georgette top but sleeveless – I don't do
sleeveless
any more – I leave that to Michelle on whom sleeveless looks good.

Pages 82 to 95 the little black dress in many variants
from short-and-tight to shorter-and-tighter –
I did shifts when Jackie did – that was then.

Page 115 – OMG! – a shot from the rear! – with come-on
over-the-shoulder smile.

After 145 pages, after all those gorgeous photographs, handsome
layouts, flawless printing,
all those beautiful women

not one in flannel pajamas.

HEAT WAVE

Fire is everywhere this year,
sweeping through Arizona's ponderosa forests,
the sun burning like a heat cannon,
dying campfires whipped to frenzies
by the wind's hot breath.

Fire of another kind has hit this city,
day after day of 95 to 100 degrees,
concrete, blacktop, brick walls hot as furnaces.
In Chicago the elderly have died like flies.

Forget this wooing of immortality:
no more beta blockers, baby aspirin,
six hour operations to remove faulty parts,
no more Vitamin E by the handful.

It's the opportunity of a lifetime.
Turn off the air conditioner,
and wait.

IV

PICASSO EATS A FISH
(photograph by David Douglas Duncan)

His eyes bulge like black balloons in a white sky.
He stares ahead, holding before him the skeleton
of a fish, headless, bits of flesh dangling from
slender bones. He picks them clean with his teeth,
so clean that color, scales, taste, smell, name
are gone. When it's bare, he lays the skeleton
on wet clay, covers it with paper, presses it down,
lifts it, leaving the deep imprint of the spine,
the fanned ribs lying like combs on either side,
making clear the bare bones of it, the necessity,
the spinal grace. He throws the skeleton away.

A NOTE TO WILLIAM CARLOS WILLIAMS
b. 1883, d. 1963

Looking for *Spring and All*
inside your book,

         and outside
for twig dogwoods reddening, yellowing,
skunk cabbages gone April-mad,
for the scratch of rakes,
wheelbarrows, red or otherwise,
(mostly otherwise and parked in mid-lawn),

inside this gift book, I turn to the fly-leaf
to find these words written to me by my son:

      For a thousand mothers,
        but to just one
          do I
       owe my life,
      give my love,
       and run.

WORDSWORTH IN SEPTEMBER

He wandered lonely as a cloud in every season,
as boy, man, revered elder – I see him
stick in hand, baggy tweeds, muddied country boots,
trudging up hill and down dale, but surely spring
was his favorite, that season of new life when
ten thousand daffodils made his heart dance,
this poet/man who believed *that ev'ry flower
enjoys the air it breathes* and *God's holy plan*
is manifest all around him violated only by
what man has made of man, spring leading into
the long summer days above the 54th parallel
when low shafts of light fractured clouds into
rainbows, again his heart leaping.

Yet in poem after poem he extols September, that season
when the wind passing through an autumnal grove creates
an impulse more profoundly dear than music of the Spring.
The thrilling song of a solitary woman reaper, *ne'er
is heard in Spring-time.* In September he saw fields of grain
as trophies of the sun, a nearby lake *fair sister of the sky.*

It was September, September, when he stood alone
on Westminster Bridge to watch dawn come over London:

> *The city now doth, like a garment, wear*
> *The beauty of the morning: silent, bare,*
> *Ships, towers, domes, theatres, and temples lie*
> *all bright and glittering in the smokeless air.*
> *E'er saw I, never felt, a calm so deep!*
> *Dear God! The very houses seem asleep;*
> *and all that mighty heart is lying still!*

ON A READING BY ADRIENNE RICH
AT UMASS-BOSTON
September 2003

Catching the coincidences of month and season,
the glorious day, a professor introduces her through
Wordsworth, the 10th floor view, all sun on water – the sea
fair sister of the sky…like a blue lake…unruffled, scattered
white boats, day sailors and sport fishermen trailing
white wakes unbroken but for islands *like bright trophies
of the sun.*

Adrienne Rich stands with her back to the 10th floor view,
a small woman in dark clothes, her knotted hands
holding her poems, her knuckles swollen and round
as drawer pulls. Her voice small and distinct, she reads
such lines as:

> *What are you going to?*
> *What we were before now, we are still*
> *…old subversive shapes…*

and a title:

> *If your name is on the list*

dark words hanging in the luminous afternoon
that lay all around us.

ON READING THOMAS MERTON

Thomas Merton, revered brother, picked his way through
the Bangkok street, ignored a leprous outstretched hand,
a cripple, a ragged old woman squatting beside the hotel
door, caught a glimpse of a matron leaving a coin in one
palm, not in another, of a young woman trailing the scent
of Magdalen. He entered the hotel, his shirt soaked, his whole
body dripping, sagging, his feet swollen in their sandals.

> *What do you do, Lord, when you are*
> *overwhelmed? The poor are always*
> *with us, but so many, so awful…*

He climbed the stairs – the elevator was not working.

> *I gave you my life. I stripped it bare to be*
> *the poorest of the poor. This is not the way?*
> *Are the ironies lost on you?*

He dropped his sweat soaked pants, shirt, shorts on the
floor of his room and showered and left the cool droplets
on his skin. Last night's poem lay on the floor beside his
bed. He leaned over, dripping on it, and read, thinking,

> *The beggars get to me. Monks, too, exist on*
> *hand-outs, or jams and jellies – stripping your life*
> *bare does nothing – the ego is still there – nothing*
> *can keep us hidden.*

Reading his lines, he thought,

> *Lord, at Bethany you inhaled the sweet perfume,*
> *felt the soft hair and the oil on your tired, encrusted*
> *feet. When Iscariot protested the waste, you*
> *brushed him aside. Burial ointment, you said,*
> *used early.*

He dripped a puddle on the floor as he read the lines,

> *O we must quickly give away our lives before one*
> *night is over – and waste our souls on him at this one*
> *supper.*

And thinking,

> *There is only one way to be poorer*
> *than the poor before you.*

He reached out to switch on the electric fan.

FOR STANLEY KUNITZ
b. July 1905, d. May 2006

Death at one hundred is not to be mourned.
This man knew life well, *the wild braid* of it,
its linear cycles, its *layers* and *litter*. He
knew it through the life of plants, of seasons,
years, their numbers mounting, each with a spring,
a summer, a fall, a winter. He held onto his own
life, coming close to letting it go: *I am not done
with my changes*, he wrote well before the last
observable one took him away.

Life at one hundred is to be celebrated, and celebrate
friends and admirers did, that summer in Provincetown's
Fine Arts Work Center, in the room named for him,
a founder. He sat before us, slumped at first; then
straightening a little, he read or spoke from memory five
or six poems, one new, before crumpling again in his chair,
adrenalin gone, the skeleton no longer supporting the body in
an upright position. The crowd, many giving him
personal greetings as they passed, drifted out into the court-
yard for wine, cheese, birthday cake, until he sat there alone.

I hesitated, then approached his chair. *It's a privilege,*
I said, *to be here for your hundredth birthday.* He lifted
his head, looked up at me with his large round black eyes.
His glance seemed to say, *I've forgotten your name…
but your face…* He had never seen me before nor I him.
For some reason I held out my hand, not to shake his so
much as to clasp fingers, to touch.

> He took my hand in his, lifted it to his lips, and kissed it.
> And I thought to myself, *Shall we get a room?*

About The Poet

I am tempted to say: *Very little more is known.* In the deepest sense this is true, but still there are the facts.

I was born north of Chicago in 1921. My pre-school years were spent with two brothers, one older and one younger, where my parents' busy household included one grandmother or the other, and the story-telling Nettie Proctor. I remember trips to Schlosser's Market, Wilson's Bakery, Zick's Department Store, to Mr. Ilg the florist, the green grocer's, the bank, the library, the railroad station; later, progressive Winnetka schools, Horace Mann Grade School, Skokie Junior High, and New Trier High School. Certain features demarcated my physical horizons – the great Lake Michigan to the east, the farmlands and great prairies to the west, the woods around our house.

As my world grew wider, Chicago was central: my father's place of business, the Blakely Printing Company on the Chicago River; the World's Fair of 1933 with its Italian airplanes and Chinese dancers; Saturday excursions to the Chicago Art Institute and the Field Museum; summer trips by car to Canadian lakes, to New Mexico; one year spent in the Ojai Valley; two years in Tucson where I graduated from high school, many visits to northern Mexico.

All this time, I was learning, observing, finding my ever-changing self, and finding my way as a writer, starting first with journalism. Wars, the loss of friends. Then love, our wildly modern house in Davenport, Iowa, my own family including three sons; my husband, Jim, our shared perspective on the world and what we should do in it.

I met Jim at the University of Chicago. He came from Miles City, Montana. We were together 49 years, from 1943 until his death in 1992, with a year and a half separation during World War II. Some of his stories of growing up in Montana in the 1930's went into my first young adult novel, *Pistol* (The New York Times 'Top Ten,' 1969). Experiences in Israel on an archaeological site became the background for the second book, *The Accomplice*; stories of my own life in my third novel, *Wings*. My sons were the models for the brothers in my fourth novel, *Into The Road*, three boys pressed into two characters.

In 1992, when Jim died, I was 70, and as the survivor, I realized I faced the re-design of my life. I wanted to get back to some creative work. I feared the long days of writing novels, closed off in my library for a year or more. I needed projects that took me out into the world, engaged me with people. The brevity of a poem appealed to me. Unlike a novel, it didn't take two years to write one.

Now, more than 20 years later, I have a body of poetry, with many rewarding moments, and many beloved friends to thank for the richness of these years. The book in your hands has come of all this.

Acknowledgments

The matter of gratitude for help, encouragement, and the care-and-feeding of the artistic spirit is a deep one that I am reminded of daily.

My mother comes to mind first: all those bedtime songs and lullabies, and later, Christina Rossetti, A. A. Milne, William Blake, Dorothy Aldis, Eugene Fields, and Robert Louis Stevenson.

At my book publisher, the Atlantic Monthly Press, my perceptive editors and lifelong friends were Nancy Beck and Emily McLeod.

From 1993, for almost a decade, I was part of the River Road Poetry Group in Westport, Massachusetts. Since 2000, I have been a member of the Black Oak Poets outside Boston.

I am particularly grateful to the poets, David Ferry, Kathleen Aguero, Patricia Cumming, and Lee Rudolph, for their critical attention and insightful readings.

Made in the USA
Charleston, SC
14 November 2013